T0208322

ONE MAN'S COINCIDENCES:

BELIEVE IT OR NOT

MICHAEL AUCLAIR

BALBOA
PRESS

A DIVISION OF HAY HOUSE

Balboa Press books may be ordered through booksellers or by contacting:

Balboa Press
A Division of Hay House
1663 Liberty Drive
Bloomington, IN 47403
www.balboapress.com
1 (877) 407-4847

Print information available on the last page.

ISBN: 978-1-9822-3072-2 (sc)
ISBN: 978-1-9822-3073-9 (e)

Balboa Press rev. date: 07/09/2019

CONTENTS

Acknowledgments xv

1. How It All Started 1

2. Drinking Stupor 2

3. On the Beach 3

4. Driving Experience 5

5. Traveling Towns 6

6. On the Road 7

7. The Hospital 8

8. Restaurant Friend 9

9. The Boat Guy.. 10

10. Bar Owner 11

11. Virginia... 12

12. My Cousin in Heaven... 13

13. Friends Together 14

14. Sunset Strip 15

15. Next-Town Girl... 16

16. Our Kids Play Sports 17

17. Under the Stands 18

18. Boy, a Car 19

19. My Boss, the Movie Star 20

20. We Always End Up Together 21

21. Driving from South Beach 22

22. Boston Connection 23

23. On the Slopes 25

24. Twins.. 26

25. Car Down and Out 27

26. Girl from South Shore....................................... 28

27. Death of a Friend 29

28. Roommate's Sister-in-Law 30

29. Same Birthdays 31

30. Marathon Girl 32

31. Bring a Date 33

32. The Hockey Friend 34

33. Girl from Work 35

34. Rowland Heights Connection 36

35. 4 in 1 37

36. Girlfriend/Cousin 38

37. Wellesley 40

38. Waltham Connection 41

39. Golfing 42

40. Hollywood to Hollywood 43

41. Doctor/Lawyer 44

42. The Delano 45

43. New England and Soccer 46

44. Dallas Cowboys 47

45. Neighbor 48

46. College 49

47. On the Plane 50

48. Store Girl and the Healer 51

49. Nightclub Connection 52

50. The News Guy 53

51. The Story 54

52. They Live Close 55

53. Billiards 56

54. Cheerleaders................................. 57

55. High School Twins 58

56. The Plate 59

57. Girl on Cape Cod 60

58. The Super Bowl Ring......................... 61

59. Ski Country 62

60. Cape Cod to Florida 63

61. Real Estate 64

62. New England Patriots Fans................... 65

63. Southern California 66

64. My Building 67

65. Bartender 68

66. Cigar Friend................................. 69

67. The Cop..71

68. Wellesley Woman 72

69. San Diego Connection....................................73

70. Police Connection..74

71. My Nurse..75

72. Georgia...76

73. Cali..77

74. Ketchup 78

75. Special New Friends..79

76. The Driving Range 80

77. The Donut Shop 81

78. Elderly Gentleman 82

79. South Carolina...83

80. The Wallet 84

81. My Keys 85

82. New Jersey 86

83. Jazz 87

My book is about several special people in my life as well as people whom I have met over the years and who sometimes intertwined with the people that I knew. I believe you will find it entertaining as I did while I was writing it to relive some of those memories.

To my readers,

I have thought about writing this book for so many years I can't even remember how long ago it was. I have started and stopped several times. I was inspired to finish it by a friend of mine who has also written a book. Thank you, Maura!

Anyone who reads this book will know if they are in it or have heard one of these stories over the years from me. I would not be surprised if they thought I was making all this up. I have hidden names and establishments sometimes to protect the guilty and the innocent. Haha. I want to thank you all for being part of my life.

This book contains stories throughout my life that would be considered coincidences. They range from mild to bizarre.

ACKNOWLEDGMENTS

Maura Lawler, for giving me the inspiration to finally finish my book.

Cheryl Auclair Miller, for the back cover photograph of the street sign with my last name on it. Thanks, my sister.

Papa Joe Vasconcellos, for his front cover photograph and for being the person who turned me on to wearing fedora hats. Thank you.

To all the people in the book for being a part of my life. You will know who you are when you read it.

HOW IT ALL STARTED

When I was young, I lived in Montebello, California. One of the boys at school was in my class from first to third grade. At the end of the third grade, my parents moved us to a faraway area called Rowland Heights. It had nothing but a large tract of new homes. There were no freeways, just a bunch of rolling hills above us. My aunt and uncle and their kids had moved around the corner also. There were a lot of children in the neighborhood, and I am still friendly with one of them to this day.

When I went into class for fourth grade, the boy who had sat next to me in first, second, and third grades was in the classroom. His parents had moved here also, and our parents didn't even know each other. It was just a coincidence. He lived next door to my relatives around the corner, and we had been there the whole summer without ever seeing each other. We ended up being in the same class for three more years before I moved to Boston.

DRINKING STUPOR

My best friend was singing during happy hour at a bar, as he normally did on Fridays at a place near Fenway Park. After he finished, we went around the corner to a place where he used to sing. That was where we had met and I used to work. We all had a pretty good buzz on.

I eventually decided to go and thought he should come with me, but he said he was okay. This must've been ten or eleven o'clock that night.

About two o'clock in the morning, my phone rang. My friend was calling. He said he had gotten pulled over.

"Where are you?"

He said he was at home and the state trooper who had pulled him over was someone I knew. I only knew one state trooper in Massachusetts. He was a friend of my roommate. The state trooper asked for his license, and when he saw it, he said, "Are you the guy who sings at that bar near Fenway Park?"

My friend said yes.

The state trooper said, "You have a friend who owns a sportswear company?"

My friend said yes.

The state trooper said, "What's his name?"

When he said my name, the state trooper told him to be careful and go home.

ON THE BEACH

I was in Florida on one of my yearly vacations. I had been going to South Florida for many years to escape the winter cold of the Northeast. On this particular day, I was sitting at a shucker bar on the beach that I had been going to for years. The guy behind the bar took my order, returned, and said, "I know you're from Boston."

I replied, "I can forget names, but most of the time, I remember faces."

He said, "Yeah, you're from Boston."

Now I was looking at my shirt to see if I was wearing a nametag or something.

He was giving me hints that he knew me, and it was driving me crazy.

After about forty-five minutes, he finally told me he was my relative's wife's nephew and had met me at a family function years ago. He'd heard I was coming to town and recognized me.

He proceeded to tell me a real whopper of a story.

He'd met two girls working at the bar, and when he was done working, they took him drinking. They got him drunk. He told me he woke up in their car in the parking lot of the hotel and there was a note telling him what room they were in. He went to the room and jumped in bed with the redhead, who rocked his world. This kid was so full of shit. What a story.

After I got home from vacation, I was at my printer when a

friend of mine walked in. We had dated in the past. She was all tanned up. I said, "Where have you been? You look great."

She said, "Florida."

I asked her what city she had been hanging out in. She mentioned a few, including Hollywood.

I said, "Hollywood? There is a great place on the beach there." I mentioned the name.

She said, "Yeah, we took the bartender and got him drunk."

I said, "You did him?"

Her eyes almost popped out of her head. We were both amazed.

Here was my chance to get even with the bullshitter. I picked up the phone, called the place, and asked for him. The receptionist told me to hold on.

Eventually, he got on the phone, and I said, "Hey, it's me. The cousin from Boston."

He said, "Hey, what's up? Are you back in Florida?"

I said, "No, I'm in Boston."

He wanted to know why I was calling him. I said, "Remember the redhead you said you did? She wants to say hello."

After she got on the phone, she started yelling that she could not believe he told anyone. She said what a jerk he was and he would never have her again.

Now at this point, I was rolling on the floor and laughing 1,500 miles away, getting even with this guy for busting my chops. Haha.

DRIVING EXPERIENCE

My best friend was singing at a big nightclub up on the North Shore, and I decide to drive up to see him. I left about ten or eleven o'clock and drove to where I worked in Boston, next to Fenway Park. It was wintertime, it was snowing, and it was cold.

I was not sure what time it was when I decided to leave and go home. I lived on the South Shore, and so did my friend, so the expressway was the way to go.

I was driving slowly when I saw a van in the breakdown lane, and I was 90 percent sure that it was my friend. There was a big Cadillac about fifty yards in front of him.

I pulled over, and as I was walking by the Cadillac, the window came down. I asked the people inside if they knew who was in the van.

A fragrance and a lot of smoke came out of the window, and the driver said no.

I walked back, and my friend was sitting in the van.

When I knock on its window, I said, "What's going on?"

He said he'd gotten a flat tire and to get in so I could warm up.

We were both a little buzzed but finally got the tire changed.

Just as were ready to leave, a state trooper pulled over to make sure we were okay, and we let him know that we'd had a flat and were leaving now.

Too funny how we ran into each other so many hours apart.

TRAVELING TOWNS

I had a passenger in my car the other day, and we started talking. It turned out she had a cousin living in Taunton, Massachusetts. I had someone close to me who played professional football and married the captain of the cheerleaders from his team, and she was from Taunton. The passenger was from the Washington, DC, area. I asked her if she knew where Glen Burnie was. She said she had a cousin who lived there too, as did my sister many years ago.

Too weird.

ON THE ROAD

I was working for a company in South Florida that sent me to California for ten days. It took me to several different cities where my company had rented office space, and I interviewed people for sales positions.

One of my stops was in Bakersfield, California, and I had a close friend who worked for the state police and traveled throughout the state to work on communication lines. He lived in Southern California, which is not even close to Bakersfield. We had been talking a couple of days before I left for my trip, and it turned out we were both going to be in Bakersfield on the same day.

So we met for dinner. Unbelievable.

THE HOSPITAL

I made a trip to Newton Wellesley Hospital to visit a friend who had had some surgery. I went into the room, and another friend of mine was in the bed next to him. They didn't even know each other! He had been brought in for an emergency. We all just laughed.

RESTAURANT FRIEND

While I was working for a company in Florida, I made a trip to California, and one of my stops brought me to San Luis Obispo. I had gotten myself a manicure and a pedicure downtown and asked the worker where I could go for something good to eat and to smoke a cigar.

I walked down the street and into the place the worker recommended, and the person behind the bar looked very familiar. I used to own a sportswear business in Boston and did custom printing and embroidery on clothing for bars and restaurants. We kept talking and trying to figure out where we knew each other from.

As it turned out, he was the general manager of a restaurant in Faneuil Hall, in Boston, that I used to do business with. We were howling. He jumped over the bar and gave me a big hug. It was crazy. We had not seen each other for years. His wife had been transferred with an airline company to this area, and he ended up running this restaurant.

Absolutely nuts.

THE BOAT GUY

When I lived in Wellesley, Massachusetts, I hung out with a group of guys who had a house at the end of a street in a small, quiet neighborhood. But this was definitely a party house, with a group of friends who hung out there almost seven days a week. We had more fun at that house than any human being should be allowed to have. I was in my early twenties, and I am still friends with those guys till this day. There were people whom I knew very well and other people who were just acquaintances.

About twenty-five years later, I'm sitting in a restaurant at a bar in South Florida, and as I look down, this face looks familiar to me. I go over and ask the person where he is from, and he says, "Wellesley."

I knew he was one of the acquaintances who used to hang out at the house. He had moved to Florida many years ago, and he was a yacht salesman. We stayed in touch for a while and then lost touch for some reason. Not sure why—just one of those things that happen in life.

BAR OWNER

In a previous story, I mentioned how I had only known one state trooper in the state of Massachusetts and that he had pulled over a friend of mine. My friend sang at a bar close to Fenway Park. As we figured it out, it was one year and one day later when the owner of that bar had closed up and was going home. I'm guessing it was probably around three in the morning. He ran a red light and got pulled over by a state trooper, who happened to be the same state trooper that I knew. When my friend explained to him what he had been doing, my state trooper friend said to him, "Is that the place where that guy sings the happy hours?"

My friend said yes. My name came up, and the owner told him, "I was the guy who made the stuff that his staff wears and the retail stuff that they sell."

This one was unbelievable.

VIRGINIA

The reason I started hanging out and eventually ended up working at the bar near Fenway Park was that I was walking by the door one night when I heard a band singing and went in. Two guys were playing acoustic guitars, and they were very good. Over time, we became very good friends, and one of them became my car insurance salesman. I went to see them one night, and one of them said to me, "We will not be here next week, as we will be singing at a Ground Round in Alexandria, Virginia."

I looked at him and said, "I will see you there."

He asked me what I was talking about. It was going to be a long weekend, with the holiday, and I had already made plans to go visit a friend of mine whom I graduated high school with and who lived in Alexandria, Virginia. My buddy and I walked in to see them play, and they couldn't believe I was there. What a howl. We had a blast.

Unfortunately, one of them passed away, but I am friends to this day with the other one.

MY COUSIN IN HEAVEN

After third grade in Montebello, California, my parents moved to an area called Rowland Heights. It was a brand-new track of homes, and there were no gas stations or highways. My cousin and his family had moved to the same area, around the corner from me. We were about the same age and became very close. When I was thirteen years old, my parents got divorced, and my mom took us to Boston. I was very sad to leave, but that's where her parents were from. Over the years, I lost touch with my cousin, but when I was twenty-one years old, I decided to go back to California, for a vacation and to get reacquainted with my dad.

I drove over to Rowland Heights to my aunt and uncle's house to find out where my cousin was and what he was doing. I had heard he was in the San Francisco area. I rang the doorbell, and my aunt answered the phone. I said, "Hi, Auntie. It's Michael Auclair," and she invited me in with big smile on her face. We talked for just a few minutes, and then I asked her about my cousin.

She said, "That's funny. He just flew in last night, and he's sleeping in the other room."

I jumped off the couch, opened the door, and jumped on him while he was sleeping. I told him who I was, but he did not remember, but when I mentioned my mother, his eyes lit up like a Christmas tree. He gave me a big hug, and we both started laughing.

I am happy to say we are still in touch with each other and close to this very day.

FRIENDS TOGETHER

On one of my many vacations to California, I put a group of us together to go to a Dodgers game. I invited a friend of my older sister to join me; we had grown up together as kids in Rowland Heights. The other two couples were a relative and his wife, along with a childhood friend and her husband. As it turns out they both lived in Corona, California.

After the game, we decided to go out to dinner. During our conversation, we discovered that both couples had lived on the same street about twenty-five years earlier, but they never knew each other. It also turns out that the girl I was with worked in the building next door to one of the gentlemen who was also at the table.

What a strange world we live in.

SUNSET STRIP

I was on vacation in California and heading into Hollywood to buy a suit for a wedding. There was an ad in the paper, and I actually ended up buying two. Afterward, I decided to head down to Sunset Strip to see it for the first time in probably twenty years. It didn't appear to have changed that much, and I decided to walk into one of the famous places there. As I started to talk to the female bartender, we realized we knew each other from a bar in Boston, next to Fenway Park, that I did business with. I could have picked any joint to walk into, but I picked this one. We had known each other for years, so we chatted about old times and Boston.

NEXT-TOWN GIRL

How about two coincidences at once? I was sitting at a bar on Hollywood Beach, and a person was standing outside the window of this location wearing a Yankees jacket. The girl sitting next to me at the bar, who was by herself, made the statement that she couldn't stand the Yankees.

I said to her, "I'd love to buy you a drink."

"You must be from Boston," she replied.

When I said yes, she told me she was from Natick, where my ex-wife was from and the town next to the one where I lived. We discovered they went to high school together.

As we were talking, I saw a girl coming down the Boardwalk whom I recognized from Cape Cod. She was the girlfriend of someone I lived with on the cape. I got out of my chair and went to the Boardwalk to say hi. Her eyes lit up, and we just started howling and laughing. She came in to join me and the girl I was talking to for a drink. She had never been to Hollywood before. After she left, the other girl and I continued to drink and talk. She had a hotel room right down the street, and we went back there and got romantic. She said she was going back to Boston the next day.

Several months later, someone who had hung around the bar for many years passed away. He was from Boston also, and we had many mutual friends. I went to the funeral, and the girl I met at the bar was there. As it turns out, she was the ex-girlfriend of the person who passed away. Really weird.

OUR KIDS PLAY SPORTS

Back in the days when we used to party on Cape Cod, where my best friend sang during happy hour, I became good friends with these four girls who would show up to the club every weekend with either their boyfriends or by themselves. Over the years, I ended up dating two of them, and one of those relationships lasted many years. They also partied up in ski country as well as at the clubs my friend sang at. One of the girls ended up marrying her boyfriend, and they are still married to this day. We stayed friends for many years and still hung out now and then. They started a family, and as we all know, you just can't go out as much after that.

Over time, we lost touch, but we reconnected on Facebook. One day I was chatting with the wife of someone I used to work for when I was the New England director for the VNEA as well as a salesman for a company in the video and entertainment industry. As it turns out, they lived in the same town, and they knew each other because their kids were involved with sports together. Sometime later, I reconnected with someone whom I went to high school with. She also lived in the town and was friends with the two other girls, whom I knew for the same reason. They all wanted to know how I knew everyone. It was pretty funny.

UNDER THE STANDS

I was planning a trip to California. When I travel there in the summertime, I always check to see where the Dodgers are playing, as I don't get to see them that often living in Florida, obviously. It turned out they were playing the Padres down in San Diego. I called Dodger Stadium to find out about tickets, and the woman on the phone gave me a number to a woman down in the stadium where the Padres played. I ended up getting a ticket in the third row behind the Padres' dugout so I could see into the Dodger dugout. LA's Orel Hershiser was pitching against Bruce Hurst, one of the all-time best left-handed pitchers for the Red Sox. I wore my Red Sox hat, and as it turned out, I was sitting next to three couples.

The girl next to me looked at me and said, "Boston, I remember Boston." She had gone to Boston College. As we talked more, it turned out she had worked as a waitress in Falmouth, Massachusetts, where I had spent several summers. I was friendly with several people who owned bars and restaurants there, and I named different people to see who she might know. When I came to one person, she looked at me and said, "Oh, I remember him. We got romantic under the stands at the BC–Wisconsin game back in the seventies."

Her husband obviously knew, because he just laughed. I couldn't believe what she was telling me. It was absolutely hysterical. I ended up going out with them after the game, and we had a great time. When I got back to Boston, I called my friend, and without even telling him the whole conversation, when I told him her name, he said, "Oh yeah, we got romantic under the stands at a BC game." Absolutely hysterical.

BOY, A CAR

I was in the parking lot of a shopping mall down here in South Florida, not too far from where I lived at that time. I was driving an old Toyota, and there was a Mercedes next to me with a for-sale sign on it. The guy who owned it was walking up to his car, and I started to ask him questions about it. He asked me if I wanted to go for a little ride and check it out, and I said yes.

It drove pretty well and was in good condition, but it was a little out of my price range. Also, I never bought a car unless it was from a dealer. I got his phone number anyway. We said goodbye, and I went to run some errands. About two hours later, I pulled up to the front of my apartment building, and the Mercedes was right in front of me, at the valet. The guy was getting out. We looked at each other and both said at the same time, "You live here?" We both said, "Yes" and started laughing. We had never seen each other there before, but he had lived there over a year. Too funny.

MY BOSS, THE MOVIE STAR

I bartended at a piano bar next to Fenway Park. Not only did I do business with the location, but I got very friendly with the owner. He was a great guy. At some point, he hired a new manager, who turned out to be an actor who had starred in a classic golf movie that remains famous to this day. The movie has a furry character in it that digs holes throughout the golf course. It was very cool. All the staff enjoyed having him as their boss. We had not seen each other in years, and I was on vacation in San Francisco when we ran into each other at a sushi bar. It was neat to catch up.

WE ALWAYS END UP TOGETHER

About twenty of us made a trip to Chicago. Someone lived there whom some of the guys went to college with. He had gotten his brother and some of their friends to chauffeur us around so we could drink and not worry about it. One day, we went to a Cubs game. We hit several bars and kept drinking. Two of the guys, who had been very good friends since they were young and hardly ever split up, went their own ways, as both had met girls and we were going to different house parties. About five hours later, they ran into each other at another house party. I was not with either one, but it was still an incredible coincidence in a story I can tell.

DRIVING FROM SOUTH BEACH

I was leaving South Beach one day, driving on Collins Avenue. I used to work on Hollywood Beach, and I knew the chief of the beach safety unit very well. I saw a Miami Beach safety unit vehicle driving, and at some point, I was able to get next to the vehicle, as the traffic was backed up. I looked over, and it was the guy who used to be the chief in Hollywood. I knew he had retired, but I did not know he had taken another job in a different city. I honked my horn, and he looked over with a big smile. We had not seen each other in years. We spoke for a minute or two before the traffic started to move. We could have been anywhere, but we ended up next to each other.

BOSTON CONNECTION

I drive for Uber and Lyft. I picked up three different passengers in a row who all had connections to Boston, where I grew up. The first one was a young female who was in town from California. She lived in Huntington Beach, where I spend most of my time when I visit California, since I grew up there and have a friend from elementary school there. She was from Wellesley, and I went to high school with her in Massachusetts. Her father was from New Bedford. She was here for one night, as she was looking at a school that she was thinking of attending, as she had graduated from college the previous year.

The conversation somehow turned to where she would live. I said she should consider living with me as a roommate. She took my card and said she was definitely interested. We shall see. Maybe she'll be my roommate before this book is published.

Next were three people who were traveling back to Massachusetts. They were from three different areas. The guy sitting next to me knew two people whom I knew, one of them from my days bootlegging T-shirts; he had sold his business to a very famous underwear company and made big bucks. There were three brothers who owned many nightclubs, bars, and restaurants that I did business within Boston, and this guy had played golf with one of the brothers in the Bahamas every day for a week. One day, they got done playing golf and gave each other a high-five. One of the brothers that I knew broke some blood vessels in the hand of this guy next to me because he high-fived him so hard.

The next couple I picked up was headed down to a concert on Fort Lauderdale Beach. The woman thought that she recognized my Boston accent as being from Boston as she. She was from Sharon, Massachusetts, and her ex-husband was from Natick, where my ex-wife was from.

ON THE SLOPES

So I am with the guys at a happy hour on Cape Cod, in Falmouth, Massachusetts. Our friend is singing. One of my buddies tells me there is a girl who is sitting with her parents that keeps looking at me. I tell him he's full of it. About ten minutes later, he tells me the same thing, so now I start to pay attention to see whether it's true. I am kind of glancing, and maybe there is something to this. I can't see myself asking her to dance while she's with her parents, but what the hey? I go over to ask her to dance, and she says yes. I ask her if she's been looking at me and, she says yes.

"Any reason why?" I asked.

She said, "I followed you around at Loon Mountain once for a half a day, watching you ski."

I could not believe what I was hearing, and I did not believe her until she described my ski outfit to a T. We got along great and started dating, as I would come to Falmouth every weekend. She lived there full time and was an EMT.

TWINS

I'm on Cape Cod, and I'm headed to happy hour, which is what we do every weekend to see my best friend perform. The place is always packed, as he is the number-one happy hour singer on Cape Cod. Hundreds of people will wait in line to get in, but luckily, the owner is a friend of mine, and I never have to wait. It's not what you know; it's who you know. Haha. There are always several friends in there, and we hang out together and have a blast. This particular afternoon, I look across the room to the far bar, and I see a friend of mine's girlfriend sitting there by herself, so I go over to say hello. She turns to me and says, "I'm not her. I'm her twin sister." I didn't even know my buddy's girlfriend had a twin.

We start drinking, and I realize she's just as much fun as her sister. I know I can hook up with her, but she has a friend, so I need a wingman. I find my buddy, who's visiting down with my friend, the singer, from Killington. We all go back to their house later on, and, well, you know what happens.

We started dating, and as it turned out, she played golf. She was the first girlfriend I ever had who played golf, and I loved it. She was a nurse. We would go golfing after work and go back to my place, and she always wore some sexy lingerie underneath her golf clothes.

What a life.

CAR DOWN AND OUT

I'm on Cape Cod in Hyannis on a Sunday afternoon. My car breaks down, and I have it towed to the nearest auto shop that is open. I have no clue what is wrong with it or whether I'm going to have to leave it and get a room. The first person who comes out is an old friend I've lost touch with and who I have not seen in years. He works there now. My luck could not have been better. He takes a look at it and is able to fix it, and I am on my way.

GIRL FROM SOUTH SHORE

I drive for Uber and Lyft. I picked up a female passenger one day, and we started chatting. She was from Scituate, Massachusetts. I used to live on the cape in Falmouth, and some of my roommates were brothers were from Scituate. One of them actually used to work for me in the liquor industry. As it turned out, this woman graduated high school with a girl who ended up marrying one of my old roommates. Her family owned a large real estate company in Scituate as well. This was the second time I'd picked up someone who went to high school with my buddy's wife.

It's a small world, after all.

DEATH OF A FRIEND

I lived in Newton Upper Falls, and my work was in West Newton. All I had to do was travel the length of Chestnut Street to get to work. One morning, I was crossing the intersection at Chestnut Street and Commonwealth Avenue. For some reason, I looked in my rearview mirror, and I saw a vehicle flipping end over end, as it had been hit going through the intersection. My friend's father was the chief of police and lived only a few houses down. I slammed on my brakes and ran to their house (as I knew his wife would be home) so they could get medical attention there immediately. When I got back to the accident, I realized there were four kids in the station wagon who were from my former neighborhood in Wellesley. One of them was in really bad shape.

Later on, I called the hospital. The nurse said to me, "I'm sorry. He is no longer with us." Such a tragedy. As I found out later, they had run a red light trying to catch up to me.

This is one coincidence I wish never happened.

ROOMMATE'S SISTER-IN-LAW

I'm at Abe and Louie's one night, which is on Boylston Street, in Boston. It's a nice restaurant where we sometimes hang out. The bartender is a friend we all know. He makes me the best espresso martinis. I'm in there with a good friend, and my best friend walks in with a bunch of his friends and the brother of a girl he is dating. He is with an attractive woman who looks very familiar to me, but I decide not to ask too many questions.

A couple of weeks later, my best friend's girlfriend has a big party at her father's cape house in New Seabury. Her brother walks in with the same girl, so now it's time to chill out and then ask her some questions. As it turns out, she is the sister-in-law of a friend of mine, whom I used to live with in Randolph, Massachusetts. Way too funny.

SAME BIRTHDAYS

I'm not sure if this qualifies as a coincidence, but up to this point, I have met eleven people in my life who have the same birthday as me, and I have dated three of them. How's this one? My stepbrother in California is the same age as me and has the same name as me, and we are both Red Sox fans, even though he grew up in California and I grew up in Boston.

MARATHON GIRL

A group of about twenty of us would always get together every year for the Boston Marathon. We would hang out on Newberry Street at several different locations. We did this for about twenty years. One year, I met a female at one of the locations. My friends were pretty drunk, so I decided to move to the other side of the room to get away from them, as they were busting my balls. I ended up leaving with her, and we ended up dating for a while. Every time I'd be out with her, if my friends were there, they would bust my chops about her, but for some reason, she really liked all of them. About six months later, after we had broken up, one of my friends, whose father owns a company that dealt with a lot of bars and restaurants, called me. He said to me," You'll never guess who's working as a secretary in my father's office." Of course, I had no clue until he told me it was the girl I used to go out with. Too funny.

BRING A DATE

My sister was engaged to a guy who lived in Mission Hill. At some point, there was going to be a get-together at another sister's house for the families to meet. I was at happy hour in Kenmore Square, watching my best friend sing. Many of the girls we hung out with were there. That day, there was a new girl in the group, and as we started talking, she told me her last name. I asked her if she was related to the person who was engaged to my sister, and she told me, "Yes, he is my brother." She was really cute, and we started dating.

The family set up the get-together at my sister's house, and we had not told our families that we were dating. We decided to tell our families we were bringing a date, and when we showed up together, everyone started howling.

THE HOCKEY FRIEND

I worked for a company called Students of America. They sold advertising on book covers and posters for educational institutions. I worked in the office, making phone calls to schools and getting them to sign up for the program. Eventually, I made a trip to California to do interviews and set up different areas. At one point, I interviewed someone who had been a former roommate of a friend of mine, who played professional hockey. Small world.

GIRL FROM WORK

I worked for a company down here in South Florida for a while, and I used to go out with a group of people after work sometimes. At some point, I had to go to a condo meeting where I was living, and one of the girls whom I worked with and who used to be in the group that went out also lived in my complex. We never knew it, and we had never seen each other.

ROWLAND HEIGHTS CONNECTION

I lived in a town called Rowland Heights in Southern California back in the sixties. The town had just formed, with a brand new track of homes. It was a bunch of rolling hills. No freeways, one store, and a gas station. It is all grown up now. It is also 100 percent Asian now.

Recently, I picked up an Asian family and took them to the port to go on a cruise. We were making small talk, and California came up as the place where they lived. I told them that I grew up in Rowland Heights, and the wife said, "That's where my parents live." Usually, nobody's even heard of Rowland Heights, even in California. Haha.

4 IN 1

How about four coincidences at once? This one is unbelievable. I picked up a woman named Sylvia (she asked me to use her real name). She was a little frantic, as she needed me to take her to pick up a cake and then add a second stop. I let her know how to add the second stop on her app. I was having dinner at 6:00 p.m. in Boca Raton, and it was 4:15, so I asked her if she was going to Miami, because in that case, I would not be able to make the trip. She said, "No, I'm going to Boca." I couldn't believe it. I was actually going to get paid to go up and see my friend for dinner.

On the trip, she told me she was in town because her niece, who was two years old, just had open-heart surgery at Joe DiMaggio hospital in Hollywood, Florida. A good friend of mine is married to the director of heart operations at Memorial Hospital. As it turned out, my friend's husband had been in the OR performing the operation. I had texted my friend to give her the name of her niece so she could check with her husband. Then she told me she was from Westwood, New Jersey. I used to run a company up in Boston that was based out of Westwood. I started to tell her about my book, and I told her I was going to put these things in it. I told her about the first story that happened to me involving Rowland Heights, California. The next town over from Rowland Heights was Hacienda Heights, and wouldn't you know it? I was dropping her off at Hacienda Circle.

GIRLFRIEND/COUSIN

I decided to become a big brother with the Jewish Big Brothers Big Sisters Association of Boston. I had filled out all the paperwork and had done my interviews and was waiting to be matched up with my little brother. Halloween was approaching, and I was dating this girl from the South Shore. She needed to babysit for her cousin a couple days before Halloween and asked me if I would join her and help him cut out a pumpkin. He was a cute little six-year-old with platinum blond hair and a smile from ear to ear. Very outgoing with a great personality. I had a blast with him.

About two weeks later, I got a call from the Big Brothers Big Sisters association that I was being matched up with my little brother. It turned out to be the same little boy I had carved the pumpkin with. We both couldn't wait to see each other, and when I showed up at his house with my social worker to meet him and his mother, I was very excited. His face lit up like a Christmas tree, and we ended up spending nine great years together. We were actually Big and Little of the Year at one point, and they sent posters throughout the with Combined Jewish Philanthropies.

There was another coincidence involving my little brother. We were out one day, spending time together, and we decided to stop for some Chinese food at a takeout place near his house. I saw a local newspaper that I had never seen before. I opened it up, and there was an article about my little brother and me. I didn't even remember being interviewed by the agency for the article, but I guess I was.

He and I were unbelievably surprised. The person at the restaurant wanted to know what we were so excited about, and when I told him, he ended up giving us the Chinese food for free, because he thought what we were doing was a great thing. Pretty awesome.

WELLESLEY

I picked up a passenger today. She was headed to the airport. We had about a ten-minute ride, so we made some small talk. I asked her where she was from, and she told me. Then she asked where I was from, and I said Boston. She said she had gone to college there, and I asked, "What college?" She said Wellesley College, which is in Massachusetts, and I said, "No kidding? I'm from Wellesley. You must have been chasing the Babson guys."

"Yeah," she said. "I married one."

Too funny.

WALTHAM CONNECTION

As I've said before, I drive for Uber and Lyft. I picked up two guys from Massachusetts who were going to the airport. One of them was from Waltham. He knew a friend of mine down here in Hollywood Beach whom he had grown up with. He did not know that my friend lived here. The other guy was from Cohasset and knew a friend of mine whom I lived with on Cape Cod. He worked for a very large real estate company in Scituate. My friend's wife's family owns a real-estate business, and this guy went to school with my friend's wife.

GOLFING

I picked up a passenger one day who was a PGA member. I love golf, so as we started to talk, he mentioned that he had been the club pro at Ocean Edge on Cape Cod. I told him I had a friend who lives there, and he said, "Yeah, he has been the club champ many years in a row."

I knew my friend and his wife from Cape Cod, as they used to come into happy hour at a popular spot on the cape. I sent a message to my friend's wife, who I knew very well, as I dated a few of her friends back in the day, telling her I had met this gentleman. I ended up putting them in touch. It is such a small world, and this was quite a coincidence.

HOLLYWOOD TO HOLLYWOOD

I have lived in Hollywood, Florida, for many years. I was on the beach hanging out one day and I found a wallet. The person lived in Hollywood, California. I ended up tracking him down and speaking with this gentleman. He was very appreciative that I had found his wallet. I got his address and mailed it from Hollywood, Florida, to Hollywood, California. Pretty funny.

DOCTOR/LAWYER

At some point, I needed hernia surgery. The injury happened while I was on the job, and I ended up having the surgery at the hernia institute in Miami. As it turned out, my doctor owned a home in New Seabury, on Cape Cod, where my attorney also owned a home. They did not know each other, but they lived on the same street, which I thought was really strange.

THE DELANO

So I'm driving down in Miami, and I have three female passengers in my car from out of state. I think it was the Carolinas. I'm kind of playing tour guide, telling her about some different places. Then I get in front of the Delano, in South Beach, and tell him that if they have a chance, they should go into this hotel, because it's absolutely fantastic and beautiful inside. Long pool and a couple of bars outback. It's my favorite place in South Beach.

Not even thirty seconds after I tell them about the Delano, I get a text from a friend of mine who lives in Massachusetts, and she says, "Not sure what your plans are, but I'm at the Delano in South Beach."

I bang the U-turn, and we end up finally reaching each other on the phone. I hang out with her and her two children, whom I have never met, outside the pool. I also see her brother, whom I have not seen in about thirty years, who is with his daughter.

We were so psyched to see each other. It was pretty awesome.

NEW ENGLAND AND SOCCER

I picked up this kid who was about twenty-two years old, and we started chatting. He was a soccer player. I picked him up about twenty minutes west of Hollywood, Florida, where he was going. I asked him why he wasn't playing soccer in Hollywood, and he said he didn't know anything about soccer there, so I told him how to look up Hollywood Parks and Recreation and find out more. I also picked up my phone and called a very good friend of mine, my mechanic, who ran a lot of the soccer in Hollywood. They talked on the phone for about five minutes, and the kid took my friend's phone number. As it turned out, he also worked at a restaurant that a friend of mine owned in Fort Lauderdale. His girlfriend was from Rhode Island, and he and his friends were all fans of the New England Patriots, who had just won the Super Bowl.

DALLAS COWBOYS

About a month ago, I picked up a passenger who was going to the airport. We started to talk sports, and it turned out he was the procurement director for the Dallas Cowboys.

Just recently, I had picked up someone going to the Miami airport who was the owner of a company running a festival in the Caribbean. As we talked, I learned he had done some other things as well as sports entertainment, and he also used to work for the Dallas Cowboys. My current passenger knew my previous one, and he was going to surprise him with a hello for me.

NEIGHBOR

I was working for a company in Florida and had to go to a seminar for training. The person sitting next to me looked familiar, but I wasn't sure from where. After talking for a while, we realize we lived in the same condo building.

COLLEGE

I was hanging out with a friend of mine one day, and he brought along someone else whom he knew. It turned out his wife went to college with my ex-wife. Really strange.

ON THE PLANE

I live in Florida. One day, I hopped on a plane to go on vacation, just to get away to relax. I was walking down the aisle, and I ran into someone who used to bartend in Boston at a place that I hung out at near Boston College. I had not seen him in years.

STORE GIRL AND THE HEALER

I picked up a passenger who was a sound meditation person. He traveled all over the world to do events for businesses in groups of people. I was very intrigued by what he did, and he was holding an event at a hotel in Fort Lauderdale. I had other plans, so I could not make it, but we stayed in touch. During a ride, we picked up another passenger who worked at a local convenience store. She was very intrigued also. About a month later, I picked her up again and called the other person so they could say hi to each other. Pretty funny.

NIGHTCLUB CONNECTION

I picked up a passenger to bring to the airport. It turned out he had gone to Boston University and was friends with an owner of a nightclub I did business within Boston. He put me on the phone with him, and we just laughed about all the great memories of the good all days. Good to be in touch with an old friend.

THE NEWS GUY

I picked up a woman going to the airport in Fort Lauderdale who was flying to Chicago. I started to talk about sports, and as it turned out, she worked for WGN in Chicago, which broadcasted sports on TV. I know the father of the head news guy at that station, and I play golf with him. Everybody knows his son in Chicago.

THE STORY

I traveled up to Boston in the summer of 2018 for a wedding. I put together a golf event the day before the wedding, with twelve guys. Some of them met each other for the first time. My best friend was part of this group. At some point, around the third or fourth hole, I told a story to a friend of mine about something really strange that happened. About five or six holes later, for some reason, my best friend started to tell the same person the same story, and they had never met before. Really strange.

THEY LIVE CLOSE

I picked up a couple of guys at a hotel in Fort Lauderdale to go to the airport. They were both from Boston, where I am from. One of them lived in Braintree and used to live next door to a friend of mine from high school. The other guy used to live in Corona, California, where I have living relatives, and he knew one of them when he lived in Corona.

BILLIARDS

Many years ago, I was the director for the VNEA in New England. This is a worldwide organization that pairs up vendors with locations to run pool leagues. I worked for a friend of mine who ran the entertainment vending company. I was traveling somewhere when I met a pool player who played in the VNEA, but not in New England. He knew the owner of the company I worked for, because they had gone to college together.

CHEERLEADERS

I picked up this passenger one day, and we started to talk. He was a good-sized gentleman and probably played football. As it turned out, he did play college ball, and he went to college with the defensive coordinator of a professional football team. Someone very close to me played for that team as well and married a cheerleader on the team. This gentleman also dated a cheerleader from the same team.

HIGH SCHOOL TWINS

I went to high school with Hungarian twins who were more than six feet eight inches tall. They lived around the corner from me, and we all hung out together in high school.

Recently, I picked up a family who was from Hungary. The man had the same name as one of the brothers of the Hungarian twins I went to high school with. As it turns out, even though he was part of a set of twins, his brother had the same name as one of the other brothers. Really strange.

THE PLATE

I was with this lady to the airport. She was from Newton, Massachusetts. As we got stuck in some traffic, I saw a Massachusetts license plate with a whale on it. My Florida license plate had a whale on it too. I had the opportunity to get next to them. I said hello and told them that I had been in Wellesley, Mass., and had a whale on my plate as well. They said they were from Newton, Mass, as was the woman in my car. You just never know.

GIRL ON CAPE COD

My best friend owned a house on Cape Cod, and I was spending the summer with him. I invited my cousin down for the weekend. We went out to one of the clubs and sat at a table. My cousin noticed this girl kept kind of walking around our table, and finally, my cousin invited her over. They hooked up and ended up leaving. Remember now that my cousins had never been to the cape to hang out with my friends and me. He showed up later at the house with the girl, and as it turned out, my best friend used to nail her, and she was none too happy to see him. All I could do was laugh my ass off. I thought it was a riot.

THE SUPER BOWL RING

So this person that I knew very well who played professional football was going to meet me in town one night for drinks in Boston. We set a time and place. I parked my car and walked toward the place. He sat down at an outdoor table with some friends. I just smiled and said, "Hi" and "I'll see you in a while." He took off his Super Bowl ring and handed it to me and said, "Here, go have fun with it." Every time I would lift my hand up to take a drink from my glass, I would do it slowly so people would notice it. I was having a blast, and I struck up a lot of conversations. He showed up, and I just kept wearing the ring, and he was laughing his ass off.

SKI COUNTRY

My best friend owned a club up in ski country. A group of girls we knew used to hang out there every weekend. My friend, who played professional football, met one of the girls in Newport, Rhode Island. I guess they started to talk, and it turned out that she knew my best friend and me, and my buddy told her that he knew us as well.

CAPE COD TO FLORIDA

My best friend and I have a friend who owned a restaurant/bar with his wife down in Woods Hole, Massachusetts. My best friend actually used to sing there for happy hours. My best friend was visiting me in Florida, and I decided to take off for Orlando for a couple of days. I ended up running into our friend and his wife in that restaurant. Way too weird.

REAL ESTATE

We were hanging out at a great steak joint in Boston, where we always used to go. A friend of mine from Cape Cod, whom I had not seen in a long time, came into the restaurant. My best friend was with me, and he knew this guy real well, as they lived near each other on the cape and were very friendly. They rode Jet Skis together, and their families hung out. I don't know how it came up, but this guy knew an old roommate of mine from Randolph, Massachusetts, because they did real estate dealings together.

NEW ENGLAND PATRIOTS FANS

I decided to go over to the Caribbean for a week. While sitting in the waiting area in Fort Lauderdale, I noticed a girl wearing a Patriots shirt and said, "Go, Patriots." There happened to be five or six different families sitting around her, and for some strange reason, they were all from the Boston area, and all Patriots fans, obviously. One of the couples was from Needham, Massachusetts, which is the town next to Wellesley, where I grew up. Someone close to me used to play for them, so I showed them some pictures. We were all just having fun talking about it.

I was at a resort on Friday night, and I ran into the couple from Needham. I told them that the person sitting next to me on the plane was also from Needham. I asked to sit down in a chair across from them, and the guy said only if I'd talk to them. I said okay and asked where they were from. "Dover, Massachusetts," they answered, which is also next to Wellesley and Needham, where the woman from the plane had gone to high school. Then the gentleman from the airport who was from Needham came walking by. There we were, five of us, from Dover, Needham, and Wellesley, all hanging out and talking in the Caribbean. Wow.

SOUTHERN CALIFORNIA

As I have mentioned a few times, someone close to me played professional football. He is retired now and living in the San Diego area. Recently, I had a passenger who was from England but raised his family in the San Diego area. As it turned out, he raised his family in the same town that the person I know lived in, and it also turned out that the person I know played on his professional football team with a player from that town. My passenger had a daughter who went to high school with that player. It's such a small world.

MY BUILDING

I recently picked up a passenger in Fort Lauderdale, Florida. The address he was going to in Hollywood, Florida, was the condo building I used to live in about fifteen years ago. This is the second coincidence that happened with this address.

BARTENDER

The first time I hung out in Killington, Vermont, with my best friend, Jim, I met a good friend of his named Bob. Bob was the bartender at a local spot up there with a very outgoing personality. The first thing I said to myself was that he would be a lifetime bartender. He was very funny, and I enjoyed his big, thick mustache. I would look forward to going to Killington just to hang with him. Over many years, Bob also bartended in Newport, Rhode Island, and was just as famous there as he was in Killington. I am from the New England area, and I have seen Bob in both places. I had recently retired and took a part-time job transporting people for a couple of companies that would be in competition with cab companies. I recently picked up a lady going to the Fort Lauderdale airport, who lived in Newport, Rhode Island. I asked her if she knew the location of a bar there and asked her if she knew Bob, and she responded that she knew him very well. She described him just as I knew him, and I asked her to please tell him I said hello.

CIGAR FRIEND

I picked up an attractive female at a beautiful high-rise condo building in downtown Fort Lauderdale. She was going to Miami Airport. We started making small talk, and restaurants came up. We mentioned a restaurant on Fort Lauderdale Beach. It turned out I knew the general manager there, and it was one of the few cigar-friendly restaurants left on Fort Lauderdale Beach. The general manager would come out with his humidor and give cigars to customers and light them. You could smoke a cigar at the bar or at the dinner table. The restaurant had fantastic food, and there was seating inside and outside. I met the GM years ago, and we hit it off right away because of our love for cigars. Unfortunately, the place is closed now. They sold it and let all the staff go. It has reopened, but no cigars are allowed. This was a disappointment to the locals and annual vacationers. The GM would always introduce me to people. I am friends with some of them on Facebook, including one couple from Massachusetts, where I am from. Great guy.

Now the conversation turned to cigars. It turned out she was the daughter of a very famous cigar maker. In fact, her last name was the name of the cigar. Her family, especially her father, was very well acquainted with the GM at the restaurant I had been talking about. I called him on my cell phone, and they talked for about twenty minutes, catching up on old times. She got his phone number so her father could call him. They talked about a lot of family stuff.

Here's the kicker: it turns out she went to Babson College, in Wellesley, Massachusetts, where I am from. I had never met anybody outside Massachusetts who went to Babson College. Two coincidences at once.

THE COP

I was out for breakfast one morning at a nice Jewish deli that we frequented. I was with a relative and a friend. We were having our normal chitchat and breakfast. My relative said hello to a friend of ours who was walking out the door. They knew each other through work. I introduced myself and our other friend at the table to this person.

The next day, I picked up a passenger. We started making small talk, and we realized we looked familiar to each other. After a while, we realize he was the person that my relative introduced me to the day before at the deli. We thought it was pretty bizarre.

WELLESLEY WOMAN

In August 2018, I spent about a month in California. It was enjoyable to see family and friends, and I drove from Carlsbad, California, all the way to Lincoln City, Oregon, at some point. One of the days I was there was the United States Surfing Championships, in Huntington Beach, California. I hung out on the pier and had a blast watching it. I had spent most of my adult life living in Boston, and I was wearing a Red Sox hat that day. I was walking on the pier when a group of people came walking toward me, all wearing Boston sports clothing. We started to talk about the Red Sox and how well they were doing, and then we got to what cities or towns everybody was from. The last woman I asked was an elderly woman who answered, "Wellesley, Massachusetts."

I said, "Where did you say you were from?" and she responded, "Wellesley."

I told her, "That's where I am from. I have never met anybody from Wellesley outside Massachusetts before." I told her that I graduated high school in 1972, and she responded, "I graduated in 1954." That was the year I was born. I got a picture of us together and put it on Facebook, as I thought it was very cool. All her friends were in disbelief.

SAN DIEGO CONNECTION

I picked up three ladies who were going to a hotel in Fort Lauderdale Florida. They were in town for a convention. We were making small talk, and somehow the conversation turned to football. One of the ladies mentioned that she was from San Diego. I let her know that someone close to me lived in that area and played professional football. She mentioned the person I knew immediately, and I asked her how she came up with that name. As it turned out, they sat on a foundation together for an ex-football player. I tried calling him on his cell phone, but we just got his voicemail. She left him an email at the same time.

"What a small world," we both said.

Well, my friend got the messages, and he was not too surprised, as he knew how many of these things happened to me over the years. We laugh about it all the time.

POLICE CONNECTION

Many years ago, I had won a three-day weekend at Disney World, Orlando. I decided to fly into South Florida at the Fort Lauderdale airport, as I knew someone down there whom I wanted to visit first before driving up to Orlando. I got a one-way car rental and dropped the car off there. One evening, I went to a location where there were several bars and restaurants. I walked into a place that had some good music playing and sat down at the bar to have a couple of drinks. A girl came over and sat down next to me. We started talking, and we were getting along pretty well. She mentioned that she and her husband were from the same town where I was visiting someone and staying. As we talked a little more, I learned that her husband worked for the person I knew. This was definitely a coincidence.

MY NURSE

Back in my late teens or early twenties, I had an operation at Beth Israel hospital. I was having back pains and saw several doctors before they found a small tumor on the base of the tube that runs from your kidney to your bladder. I had complications the night of the surgery and ended up spending a few weeks in the hospital. At that time, they had something called primary-care nursing. I had the same nurse every day during the shift when she was working. She was extremely attractive and was very nice. I ended up giving my room to someone else who needed a room with oxygen, and I became friendly with the family. We lost touch after many years. I still kept the same primary-care nurse.

About six months later, I was coming home from work one morning. At that time, I worked from nine in the evening until five in the morning. I lived on the South Shore. It was snowing but not very heavily, and as I was crossing an intersection in my neighborhood down the street from where I lived, I had to swerve out of the way of someone who was backing out of their driveway. My car spun in circles, and she came running over to make sure I was okay. It was my primary-care nurse at Beth Israel hospital. She lived six or seven houses from me, and I had never seen her before. We had both lived there for years. We ended up going skiing a few times together, but nothing ever materialized.

GEORGIA

This might be the most bizarre coincidence of them all. It was spring break down here in Fort Lauderdale, Florida. I picked up a passenger who went to the University of Georgia and was here on spring break. We were talking about how different schools have different spring breaks. He said his sister, who went to Georgia Southern, was starting her spring break just as he was ending his. The next day, I picked up two very attractive blondes at Fort Lauderdale airport. They were from Georgia, and one of them went to Georgia Southern. It was his sister. Absolutely unbelievable.

CALI

I am in a FedEx print store to get my contract printed for my book. There is a woman at the counter before me, and I hear her say her name—Susan, the same as my sister. I hear her say she is from California, where I am from. She finishes up, and the gentleman is printing my paperwork. She says, "How do I get an Uber?"

I say to her, "I am in Uber driver."

She beeps for a driver, and it ends up being me. As we're driving, she says she lives in Cathedral City, where my aunt used to live. Her husband is from Huntington Beach, California, where I spent most of my childhood and where I still have a great elementary school friend.

We both laugh about this stuff as I take her to the hotel.

KETCHUP

A woman gets in my car. I smell food. I say, "Smells good. Is it ketchup?"

She says, "Yes, and fries also."

Thirty seconds later, a song comes on the radio. The first line of the song says, "I got ketchup on my leg."

We both start laughing.

SPECIAL NEW FRIENDS

As I've mentioned several times, someone very close to me lives in the San Diego area and is originally from California. He married a girl from Massachusetts, and I met her parents at the wedding (it was a three- or four-day wedding) in California. They were incredibly nice people, and we hit it off right away. I was happy he was getting such great, cool in-laws. About a year later, when I was working in Hollywood Beach, Florida, I was driving my pick-up truck down the Boardwalk, which has a bike lane and brick pavers and runs the length of the beach, with a whole bunch of bars, restaurants, businesses, hotels, houses, and condos. As I was passing by a great restaurant/bar that was also a Boston hangout, this guy was walking out of it toward me in my truck. I did a double take: it was my friend's father-in-law, and he had a big smile on his face. I stopped my truck and got out, and we gave each other a big hug. His wife was behind him and gave me a hug as well. I couldn't believe they were in Hollywood, Florida. They had come for a vacation and wanted to surprise me, and as he saw me driving in my pick-up truck, he had not had a chance yet to call me yet. We all laughed so hard, and I was so happy to spend a good amount of time with them while they were here. We are all very good friends these days. They are the nicest people out there.

THE DRIVING RANGE

I was at the driving range once with two other friends. We stood facing out toward the signs. One of my friends, who was tall, was on the right of me, and my other friend, who was shorter, was on the left. We were all driving balls when we saw that the cart was getting closer to us, picking up balls out there. I hit a ball, and it hit the cart and came back. My short friend, who was behind me, was bending over to put a ball on the tee, and my ball came back and hit the side of his nose and bent it to the side of his face. We heard the thump and could hear him mumbling as his blood was pouring down. We couldn't believe it. We rushed him to the hospital. Something like that couldn't happen again in a million years.

THE DONUT SHOP

I was at the donut shop once in Natick, Massachusetts, and for some reason this kid was giving me a hard time—I can't remember for what reason. A few years later, I was at a Red Sox game with a few friends. We hopped on the trolley to come home, as we lived in Newton, Massachusetts, at the time. I turned around, and there was the same kid, sitting in the back of the trolley. I got up, and I sat down right in front of him. I turned around and looked at him, and I said, "You probably do not recognize me, but I'm going to refresh your memory." I told him the story, and he denied it. I think he got a little nervous for some reason, so he got off the trolley, and I knew he would be hitchhiking on Route 9 to get up to Natick. We got off at the next stop, where my car was. We circled around and started coming up Route 9, and there he was, hitchhiking. As I drove by, he spat on my windshield. That was enough. I pulled over and chased him. That is all. Haha.

ELDERLY GENTLEMAN

I met a person the other day who was 104 years old. He owned a grocery store on Martha's Vineyard, which I believe I had been to before, as I spent many summers in Falmouth, right across the water from there. He was a very nice guy. We chatted about several things that we knew about the area. Later on, I found out that a friend of mine whose parents own a produce business were friends with this gentleman's family. Such a small world.

SOUTH CAROLINA

I picked up this couple that was going to the airport. They told me they were from Charleston, South Carolina. I told them I had a cousin who lived in Hanahan, South Carolina. The gentleman asked me if I wouldn't mind telling him his name, and I told him. The wife said three times, "What did you just say what did you just say what did you just say?" She had just had lunch, worked out, and played racquetball with my cousin two days earlier. I put them on the phone together, and everyone laughed so hard. Unbelievable!

THE WALLET

I was out with a friend of mine one night, and we had a few drinks in a place where he sang and I worked out. We decided to take a trip from Boston to Salem, Massachusetts, and head out there for a while. We ended up back at the same bar where we started at, and we had, I guess you could say, a slight buzz on. We got into his car, and I dropped my wallet in the gutter at the front door of this place. I knew I had dropped it, but for some reason, I didn't pick it up, and I didn't realize it was missing until the following morning. I drove down there, and there it was. Was I lucky—or was this another coincidence?

MY KEYS

I drove from Framingham, Massachusetts, to Nantasket Beach one night with a lady friend. It was another time when you could say I had a little buzz on. We were running in the sand on the beach, and I heard my keys fall out of my sweatshirt pocket, but I kept running. I didn't realize it until I got home. I dropped her off. I went home and used my spare set of keys to grab the flashlight, and then I drove all the way back to the beach. It took me an hour, but I found my keys. Once again, was I lucky, or was this a coincidence? Haha.

NEW JERSEY

I picked up this couple going to the Miami airport from Fort Lauderdale. As we chatted on our way, they mentioned that they had both grown up in New Jersey, in different towns, and had met through business. Although they did not know it until after they were dating for a while, their parents all went to the same high school in New Jersey together and graduated together.

JAZZ

I picked up a gentleman one day in Fort Lauderdale and traveled about forty-five minutes north. It turned out he was from California, where I grew up as a youngster, and he was in the entertainment business, as was someone close to me who lived out in California as well. I had heard of this guy before but hadn't realized how famous he was. I mentioned the person I knew in California, and he recognized his name and thought that their agents probably knew each other. He was a saxophone player and the leader of a band that was doing a Christmas tour and had a show at the Parker Playhouse. Really nice guy.

About four hours later, I picked up a guy in Fort Lauderdale who was going to the movie theater in Hollywood. As we were talking, I asked him if he had the day off, since it was midweek and he was headed to the movies. He let me know he was in town to perform in a Christmas show. I said to him, "You don't mean with so and so."

"Yeah," he said, "I'm his drummer."

Too funny.

Printed in the United States
By Bookmasters